T0045643

About Pfeiffer

Pfeiffer serves the professional development and hands-on resource needs of training and human resource practitioners and gives them products to do their jobs better. We deliver proven ideas and solutions from experts in HR development and HR management, and we offer effective and customizable tools to improve workplace performance. From novice to seasoned professional, Pfeiffer is the source you can trust to make yourself and your organization more successful.

Essential Knowledge Pfeiffer produces insightful, practical, and comprehensive materials on topics that matter the most to training and HR professionals. Our Essential Knowledge resources translate the expertise of seasoned professionals into practical, how-to guidance on critical workplace issues and problems. These resources are supported by case studies, worksheets, and job aids and are frequently supplemented with CD-ROMs, websites, and other means of making the content easier to read, understand, and use.

Essential Tools Pfeiffer's Essential Tools resources save time and expense by offering proven, ready-to-use materials—including exercises, activities, games, instruments, and assessments—for use during a training or team-learning event. These resources are frequently offered in looseleaf or CD-ROM format to facilitate copying and customization of the material.

Pfeiffer also recognizes the remarkable power of new technologies in expanding the reach and effectiveness of training. While e-hype has often created whizbang solutions in search of a problem, we are dedicated to bringing convenience and enhancements to proven training solutions. All our e-tools comply with rigorous functionality standards. The most appropriate technology wrapped around essential content yields the perfect solution for today's on-the-go trainers and human resource professionals.

Pfeiffer
www.pfeiffer.com

Essential resources for training and HR professionals

Trouble on the Inca Trail

Participant's Workbook

Lorraine L. Ukens

Pfeiffer
A Wiley Imprint
www.pfeiffer.com

Copyright © 2005 by John Wiley & Sons, Inc.

Published by Pfeiffer
An Imprint of Wiley
989 Market Street, San Francisco, CA 94103-1741 www.pfeiffer.com

No part of this publication may be reproduced, stored in a retrieval system, or transmitted in any form or by any means, electronic, mechanical, photocopying, recording, scanning, or otherwise, except as permitted under Section 107 or 108 of the 1976 United States Copyright Act, without either the prior written permission of the Publisher, or authorization through payment of the appropriate per-copy fee to the Copyright Clearance Center, Inc., 222 Rosewood Drive, Danvers, MA 01923, 978-750-8400, fax 978-646-8600, or on the web at www.copyright.com. Requests to the Publisher for permission should be addressed to the Permissions Department, John Wiley & Sons, Inc., 111 River Street, Hoboken, NJ 07030, 201-748-6011, fax 201-748-6008, e-mail: permcoordinator@wiley.com.

For additional copies/bulk purchases of this book in the U.S. please contact 800-274-4434.
Pfeiffer books and products are available through most bookstores. To contact Pfeiffer directly call our Customer Care Department within the U.S. at 800-274-4434, outside the U.S. at 317-572-3985 or fax 317-572-4002 or www.pfeiffer.com.
Pfeiffer also publishes its books in a variety of electronic formats. Some content that appears in print may not be available in electronic books.

ISBN: 0-7879-7603-2

Acquiring Editor: Martin Delahoussaye
Director of Development: Kathleen Dolan Davies
Developmental Editor: Susan Rachmeler
Editor: Rebecca Taff
Senior Production Editor: Dawn Kilgore
Marketing Manager: Jeanenne Ray
Manufacturing Supervisor: Bill Matherly

Printed in the United States of America

Printing 10 9 8 7

Contents

Trouble on the Inca Trail **1**

The Situation **1**

Your Task **2**

Guidelines for Reaching Consensus **8**

Group's Task **9**

Answers and Rationale **11**

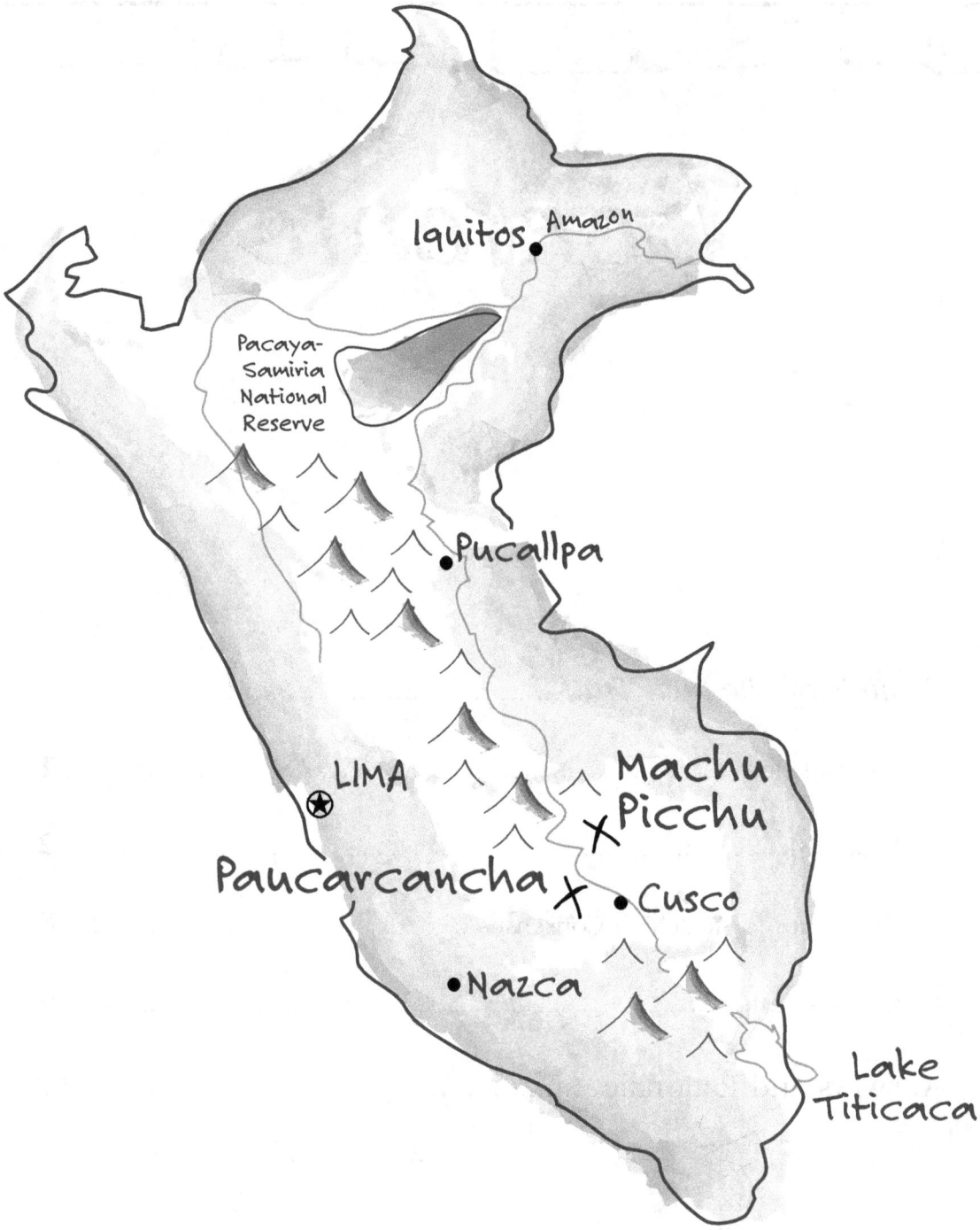
Iquitos
Amazon
Pacaya-
Samiria
National
Reserve
Pucallpa
LIMA
Machu
Picchu
Paucarcancha
Cusco
Nazca
Lake
Titicaca

Trouble on the Inca Trail

THE SITUATION

You and a small group of friends are embarking on an extended trek across Peru that will follow along the famous Inca Trail. In ancient times, the Trail was used to connect all four corners of the Incan Empire. Your route will begin in Nazca, head east to Cusco, and then move north to Iquitos. The journey will take you through three diverse ecological zones until your travels end at the isolated and primitive Pacaya-Samiria National Reserve, known to natives as the "jungle of mirrors." You will be traversing the desolate, dry Pacific coastal desert in the west; move across the centrally located, sometimes snow-capped Andes Mountains; and finally move into the lush tropical rainforest region of the Amazon Basin in northeastern Peru.

The famous Inca Trail has a well-earned reputation for the variety of flora and fauna encountered, with landscapes that run up the pass at 4,000 meters above sea level and then along a path overwhelmed by steamy jungle vegetation. Along the way, you will walk past mysterious archaeological sites half-hidden in thick undergrowth, including Machu Picchu, the "Lost City of the Incas," which is one of the world's most breathtaking sites. You will be one of the thousands who flock from all over the world to have a first-hand experience of the same trail that the Incas walked more than five hundred years ago.

Although the best time to walk the Inca Trail is from May to October, the group has decided to make its trip during April before the peak tourist season begins. However, you realize that this is a time when fewer people travel the Trail and that any problems may isolate you in any of the various locations you encounter. Most of the trail is fairly safe, but it should not be taken lightly. Some stretches wind past high cliffs, and it is easy to get lost or fall off the trail. You have made your preparations, and now it is time for the expedition to begin.

YOUR TASK

Do not communicate with anyone else. Read the predicaments that follow, choose the best answer from the three alternatives provided in each case, and write the letter (a, b, or c) that corresponds to your answer in the space provided under the heading "Your Answer." You will have fifteen minutes to complete the task, and the facilitator will give you a two-minute warning before time expires.

Predicament	***Your Answer***	***Group's Answer***	***Correct Answer***
1. You start your trip in the dry coastal desert region of Nazca, and as your proceed, the day becomes dry and extremely hot. You have with you a full canteen of water (approximately one liter) that must last you until you reach Cusco two days from now. You decide to:	_____	_____	_____
a. drink as much water as you think you need before you begin to feel thirsty.			
b. ration the water, allowing for only one cup each day.			
c. not have any water until you stop for the night, and then drink what you feel you need.			

Predicament	*Your Answer*	*Group's Answer*	*Correct Answer*
2. As the sweltering day drags on, you begin to suffer from cramps, dizziness, and profuse sweating. You recognize these symptoms as heat exhaustion and know that in order to prevent further distress you need to:	_____	_____	_____
a. move about very slowly until the symptoms subside.			
b. eat a chocolate bar.			
c. drink some lightly salted water.			
3. Two days later you arrive in Cusco and spend the night preparing for your expedition. After a restful night, early the next morning you make your way toward the archaeological ruins of Paucarcancha. When you reach them later that afternoon, you begin your explorations, but realize that there is definite danger in encountering snakes that inhabit the building remnants and natural outcroppings of the area. The best way to avoid snakes and potential harm is to:	_____	_____	_____
a. make a lot of noise.			
b. walk softly and quietly.			
c. wait until early evening.			

Predicament	*Your Answer*	*Group's Answer*	*Correct Answer*
4. You have settled into camp for the night, and you are preparing a meal for the evening. As you are removing a pot from the campfire, you realize that you are too close to the flame and your shirt sleeve has ignited. You quickly put out the fire, but you have suffered a rather severe burn. The best way to treat the burn and keep it from becoming infected is to:	_____	_____	_____
a. apply antiseptic ointment.			
b. remove any adhered particles of charred clothing.			
c. soak your arm in the nearby mountain stream.			
5. It is soon morning and you have survived the night without further difficulty. After several hours of walking inland, you find yourself at the foot of the Andes Mountains. From here the trail ascends steeply; you must now begin your route up on the mossy, slippery rock. The safest approach would be to:	_____	_____	_____
a. keep your boots on for the ascent.			
b. proceed with only your socks on.			
c. go up the rocks in your bare feet.			

Predicament	*Your Answer*	*Group's Answer*	*Correct Answer*
6. You have reached the summit and the air is crisp and clear. You realize that you are about to spend your first evening in the mountains, and you decide to go out on a brief foraging trip. As you try to make your way back to the campsite, your flashlight starts to glow dimly. Your surroundings are unfamiliar to you and the pitch dark of a moonless night is descending quickly. You should:	_____	_____	_____
a. put the batteries under your armpits to warm them for a while and then replace them in the flashlight.			
b. alternate the process of shining your light for a few seconds to get the scene in mind and then moving carefully forward into the darkness for a while.			
c. head back at once, clicking the light off and on, and hoping the flashlight will glow enough for you to make out landmarks.			
7. You awaken refreshed after a good night's rest. After walking along the main trail most of the day, you decide to try to locate a more scenic, yet less-traveled alternate route. You have enjoyed the sights and now start to head back toward the central trail. You realize that you have gone farther than anticipated, and you still have not located the trail after the sun dips below the horizon. Night begins to fall and your flashlight batteries finally wear down completely. You know that you should be heading east, but you are unsure of your current direction. You decide to rely on your knowledge of celestial navigation by observing the:	_____	_____	_____
a. North Star.			
b. Southern Cross.			
c. moon.			

Predicament	*Your Answer*	*Group's Answer*	*Correct Answer*
8. You feel relieved when you find your way back to camp as the wind suddenly begins to howl. You quickly retreat to your tent for the night and pull the flap tightly closed. You have a small stove burning inside to keep you warm. However, you need to keep a close eye on it because there is a danger of carbon monoxide if the flame begins to glow:	_____	_____	_____
a. red.			
b. yellow.			
c. blue.			
9. The next morning is bright and clear as you reach the ancient ruins of Machu Picchu. After spending several hours visiting the Inca site, you begin the descent from the mountainous area on your way toward Iquitos near the Amazon River. Before making camp for the evening, you must cross a stream that is about waist deep and has a strong current. To get safely across, you should face:	_____	_____	_____
a. upstream.			
b. downstream.			
c. across the stream.			
10. After several days, your journey has finally taken you into the tropical rainforest region of the Amazon Basin. After walking all day, you are tired and begin to think about preparing for your first night in the jungle. The most important thing now is to set up camp:	_____	_____	_____
a. near a source of water.			
b. at the base of a large tree for protection.			
c. no later than 4:00 in the afternoon.			

Predicament	*Your Answer*	*Group's Answer*	*Correct Answer*
11. The following day takes you deeper into the jungle, and you see a variety of plants and birds that you have never seen before. You come to a murky stream that must be crossed in order to proceed through an area of less dense vegetation. As you emerge from the water, you look down to see that a leech has attached itself to your leg. The best way to remove the leech is to:	_____	_____	_____
a. apply iodine.			
b. cover it with coffee grounds.			
c. pull it off with a quick and firm motion.			
12. You continue walking for most of the day and make it to the edges of the Reserve. You are reaching the last part of your trek when you step into some densely covered undergrowth. You feel a soft ooze begin to suck at your ankles, and then suddenly you find yourself standing in sand up to your knees. You realize it is quicksand! You should:	_____	_____	_____
a. fall flat on your back and float.			
b. try to swim out.			
c. stand absolutely still.			

Individual Score = _____

Average Individual Score = _____

Total Group Score = _____

GUIDELINES FOR REACHING CONSENSUS

Your group will supply a number of resources that each member lacked when you worked independently on the task. Enter into the group task with a commitment to use these resources and arrive at the best possible solutions. Shoulder your share of the responsibility for the group's success, and discuss the task and process openly and candidly. Use flexible patterns of communication so that all members of your group will be able to participate equally and will feel free to speak up when they have a need to do so. Minority opinions should be encouraged; not only will this increase participation, but it could supply information or logic that previously was missing.

The following guidelines will help during the decision-making process:

1. *Think through your own ideas* as well as you can before meeting with the group (but realize that others may know information that you do not).

2. *Express your own opinions and explain yourself fully,* so that the rest of the group has the benefit of all members' thinking.

3. *Listen to the opinions and feelings of all other group members* and be ready to modify your own position on the basis of logic and understanding.

4. *Avoid arguing for your own position* in order to "win" as an individual; what is "right" is the best collective judgment of the group as a whole.

5. *View disagreements or conflict as helping to clarify the issue,* rather than as hindering the process. Do not "give in" if you still have serious reservations about an issue; instead, work toward resolution.

6. *Recognize that tension-reducing behaviors, such as laughing or kidding, can be useful,* as long as meaningful conflict is not smoothed over prematurely.

7. *Refrain from conflict-reducing techniques,* such as voting, averaging, trading, compromising, or giving in to keep the peace.

8. *Monitor interactions among people* as the group attempts to complete its work and initiate discussions of what really is going on.

9. *Do not assume that an answer is correct* just because there is agreement initially. Discuss the reasons for the answer and explore all possibilities.

GROUP'S TASK

This task is similar to the task you performed individually, but it will be shared by your whole group. Assume that the entire group faces each predicament. The group task will be an exercise in group decision making, and your group will employ the group-consensus method in reaching its decisions. In many cases, a consensus will be difficult to reach. Therefore, not every answer may meet with everyone's *complete* approval, but each answer must be one that every member is willing to accept. When a consensus decision has been reached for each predicament, write the letter (a, b, or c) that corresponds to the answer your group selected in the space provided under the heading "Group's Answer." Leave the "Correct Answer" space blank until the facilitator gives you scoring instructions. You will have approximately one-half hour for the group task.

Answers and Rationale